TO

_____

FROM

_____

365 DAY BRIGHTENERS™

from
GOD'S WORD

*Promises and Blessings
from Scripture*

365 Day Brighteners™ from God's Word:
Promises and Blessings from Scripture
Copyright © 2004 DaySpring® Cards, Inc.
Published by Garborg's®, a brand of DaySpring® Cards, Inc.
Siloam Springs, Arkansas
www.dayspring.com

Scripture quotations are from the following sources: The HOLY
BIBLE, NEW INTERNATIONAL VERSION® (NIV®) © 1973, 1978,
1984 by International Bible Society. Used by permission of
Zondervan Publishing House. THE MESSAGE © Eugene H. Peterson
1993, 1994, 1995. Used by permission of NavPress Publishing Group.
All rights reserved. The Living Bible (TLB) © 1971 by permission of
Tyndale House Publishers, Inc., Wheaton, IL. The Holy Bible, New
Living Translation (NLT) © 1996 by permission of Tyndale House
Publishers, Inc., Wheaton, IL. The NEW AMERICAN STANDARD
BIBLE® (NASB) © The Lockman Foundation 1960, 1962, 1963, 1968,
1971, 1972, 1973, 1975, 1977, 1995. Used by permission.
(www.Lockman.org). The New King James Version (NKJV) © 1982,
Thomas Nelson, Inc. The New Revised Standard Version of the Bible
(NRSV) © 1989 Division of Christian Education, National Council of
Churches. Used by permission of Zondervan Publishing House.

ISBN 1-58061-967-3

Printed in China

365 DAY

BRIGHTENERS™

from
GOD'S WORD

Promises and Blessings
from Scripture

How many are your works, O Lord!
In wisdom you made them all; the earth is
full of your creatures.... These all look to you
to give them their food at the proper time....
May the glory of the Lord endure forever;
may the Lord rejoice in his works.

PSALM 104:24,27,31 NIV

JANUARY 1

God's blessing makes life rich;
nothing we do can improve on God.

PROVERBS 10:22 THE MESSAGE

JANUARY 2

The Lord is gracious and merciful,
slow to anger and abounding in steadfast
love. The Lord is good to all, and his
compassion is over all that he has made....
The Lord is faithful in all his words,
and gracious in all his deeds.

PSALM 145:8-9,13 NRSV

JANUARY 3

You're my place of quiet retreat; I wait
for your Word to renew me...therefore
I lovingly embrace everything you say.

PSALM 119:114,119 THE MESSAGE

JANUARY 4

I call on you, O God, for you will answer
me; give ear to me and hear my prayer.
Show the wonder of your great love....
Keep me as the apple of your eye;
hide me in the shadow of your wings.

PSALM 17:6-8 NIV

JANUARY 5

Teach us to number our days aright,
that we may gain a heart of wisdom....
Satisfy us in the morning with your
unfailing love, that we may sing
for joy and be glad all our days.

PSALM 90:12,14 NIV

JANUARY 6

Oh, I'll guard with my life what you've
revealed to me, guard it now, guard it ever;
and I'll stride freely through wide
open spaces as I look for your truth
and your wisdom; then I'll tell the world
what I find, speak out boldly in public,
unembarrassed. I cherish your
commandments—oh, how I love them!—
relishing every fragment of your counsel.

PSALM 119:44-48 THE MESSAGE

JANUARY 7

In everything you do, put God first,
and he will direct you and crown
your efforts with success.

PROVERBS 3:6 TLB

JANUARY 8

Praise be to the Lord, for he has heard my cry for mercy. The Lord is my strength and my shield; my heart trusts in him, and I am helped. My heart leaps for joy and I will give thanks to him in song.

PSALM 28:6-7 NIV

JANUARY 9

Why is everyone hungry for more?...
I have God's more-than-enough, more joy
in one ordinary day.... At day's end
I'm ready for sound sleep, for you, God,
have put my life back together.

PSALM 4:6-8 THE MESSAGE

JANUARY 10

May God be gracious to us and bless
us and make his face shine upon us,
that your ways may be known on earth,
your salvation among all nations.

PSALM 67:1-2 NIV

JANUARY 11

Mark a life of discipline and live wisely;
don't squander your precious life. Blessed the
man, blessed the woman, who listens to me,
awake and ready for me each morning,
alert and responsive as I start my day's work.
When you find me, you find life, real life,
to say nothing of God's good pleasure.

PROVERBS 8:33-35 THE MESSAGE

JANUARY 12

The Lord is the strength of his people,
a fortress of salvation for his anointed one.
Save your people and bless your inheritance;
be their shepherd and carry them forever.

PSALM 28:8-9 NIV

JANUARY 13

You've always been great toward me—what love!… You, O God, are both tender and kind, not easily angered, immense in love, and you never, never quit.

PSALM 86:13,15 THE MESSAGE

JANUARY 14

Your decrees are the theme of my song wherever I lodge. In the night I remember your name, O Lord, and I will keep your law. This has been my practice: I obey your precepts.

PSALM 119:54-56 NIV

JANUARY 15

The wise in heart are called discerning,
and pleasant words promote instruction.

PROVERBS 16:21 NIV

JANUARY 16

I will exalt you, my God the King; I will praise your name forever and ever. Every day I will praise you and extol your name forever and ever. Great is the Lord and most worthy of praise; his greatness no one can fathom.

PSALM 145:1-3 NIV

JANUARY 17

Don't you see that children are God's best gift? the fruit of the womb his generous legacy? Like a warrior's fistful of arrows are the children of a vigorous youth. Oh, how blessed are you parents, with your quivers full of children! Your enemies don't stand a chance against you; you'll sweep them right off your doorstep.

PSALM 127:3-5 THE MESSAGE

JANUARY 18

You are my portion, O Lord; I have promised to obey your words. I have sought your face with all my heart; be gracious to me according to your promise. I have considered my ways and have turned my steps to your statutes.

PSALM 119:57-59 NIV

JANUARY 19

My child, do not let these escape from
your sight: keep sound wisdom
and prudence, and they will be life for your
soul and adornment for your neck.

PROVERBS 3:21-22 NRSV

JANUARY 20

How can I repay the Lord for all his goodness to me? I will lift up the cup of salvation and call on the name of the Lord. I will fulfill my vows to the Lord in the presence of all his people.

PSALM 116:12-14 NIV

JANUARY 21

May the Lord make you increase,
both you and your children.
May you be blessed by the Lord,
the Maker of heaven and earth.

PSALM 114:14-15 NIV

JANUARY 22

I will extol the Lord with all my heart....
Great are the works of the Lord;
they are pondered by all who delight in them.
Glorious and majestic are his deeds,
and his righteousness endures forever.

PSALM 111:1-3 NIV

JANUARY 23

Telling the truth gives a man great
satisfaction, and hard work returns
many blessings to him.

PROVERBS 12:14 TLB

JANUARY 24

O Lord our God, you answered them;
you were to Israel a forgiving God, though
you punished their misdeeds. Exalt the Lord
our God and worship at his holy mountain,
for the Lord our God is holy.

PSALM 99:8-9 NIV

JANUARY 25

If your law had not been my delight,
I would have perished in my affliction.
I will never forget your precepts, for by them
you have preserved my life. Save me, for I am
yours; I have sought out your precepts....
To all perfection I see a limit; but your
commands are boundless.

PSALM 119:92-94,96 NIV

JANUARY 26

Sing to the Lord a new song, for he has
done marvelous things; his right hand and
his holy arm have worked salvation for him.
The Lord has made his salvation known and
revealed his righteousness to the nations.

PSALM 98:1-2 NIV

JANUARY 27

The Lord will keep you from all harm—
he will watch over your life; the Lord
will watch over your coming and going
both now and forevermore.

PSALM 121:7-8 NIV

JANUARY 28

Sing God a brand-new song! Earth
and everyone in it, sing! Sing to God—
worship God! Shout the news of his victory
from sea to sea, take the news of his glory
to the lost, news of his wonders to one
and all! For God is great, and worth
a thousand Hallelujahs. His terrible
beauty makes the gods look cheap.

PSALM 96:1-4 THE MESSAGE

JANUARY 29

Lord, you have been our dwelling place throughout all generations. Before the mountains were born or you brought forth the earth and the world, from everlasting to everlasting you are God.

PSALM 90:1-2 NIV

JANUARY 30

Bring joy to your servant,
for to you, O Lord, I lift up my soul.
You are forgiving and good, O Lord,
abounding in love to all who call to you.

PSALM 86:4-5 NIV

JANUARY 31

I will praise you with the harp for your
faithfulness, O my God; I will sing praise
to you with the lyre, O Holy One of Israel.
My lips will shout for joy when I sing praise
to you—I, whom you have redeemed.

PSALM 70:22-23 NIV

FEBRUARY 1

Give instruction to a wise man,
and he will be still wiser; teach a just man,
and he will increase in learning.

PROVERBS 9:9 NKJV

FEBRUARY 2

I have seen you in the sanctuary and beheld
your power and your glory. Because your love
is better than life, my lips will glorify you.
I will praise you as long as I live,
and in your name I will lift up my hands.

PSALM 63:2-4 NIV

FEBRUARY 3

Blessed are they whose ways are blameless,
who walk according to the law of the Lord.
Blessed are they who keep his statutes
and seek him with all their heart. They
do nothing wrong; they walk in his ways.

PSALM 119:1-3 NIV

FEBRUARY 4

May all who seek you rejoice and be glad
in you; may those who love your salvation
always say, "The Lord be exalted!"
Yet I am poor and needy; may the Lord
think of me. You are my help and
my deliverer; O my God, do not delay.

PSALM 40:16-17 NIV

FEBRUARY 5

The Lord is enthroned as King forever.
The Lord gives strength to his people;
the Lord blesses his people with peace.

PSALM 29:10-11 NIV

FEBRUARY 6

You turned my wailing into dancing;
you removed my sackcloth and clothed
me with joy, that my heart may sing
to you and not be silent. O Lord my God,
I will give you thanks forever.

PSALM 30:11-12 NIV

FEBRUARY 7

I have not departed from your laws,
for you yourself have taught me.
How sweet are your words to my taste,
sweeter than honey to my mouth!
I gain understanding from your precepts;
therefore I hate every wrong path.

PSALM 119:102-104 NIV

FEBRUARY 8

To you, O Lord, I lift up my soul;
in you I trust, O my God…. Remember,
O Lord, your great mercy and love,
for they are from of old. Remember
not the sins of my youth and my rebellious
ways; according to your love remember me,
for you are good, O Lord.

PSALM 25:1-2,6-7 NIV

FEBRUARY 9

A wise person gets known for insight;
gracious words add to one's reputation.

PROVERBS 16:21 THE MESSAGE

FEBRUARY 10

I am like an olive tree flourishing in the house of God; I trust in God's unfailing love for ever and ever. I will praise you forever for what you have done; in your name I will hope, for your name is good. I will praise you in the presence of your saints.

PSALM 52:8-9 NIV

FEBRUARY 11

O Lord, our Lord, how majestic is your
name in all the earth! You have set your glory
above the heavens. From the lips of children
and infants you have ordained praise.

PSALM 8:1-2 NIV

FEBRUARY 12

My soul finds rest in God alone;
my salvation comes from him.
He alone is my rock and my salvation;
he is my fortress, I will never be shaken....
Find rest, O my soul, in God alone;
my hope comes from him.

PSALM 62:1-2,5 NIV

FEBRUARY 13

God's love is meteoric, his loyalty astronomic, his purpose titanic, his verdicts oceanic. Yet in his largeness nothing gets lost…. How exquisite your love, O God! How eager we are to run under your wings.

PSALM 36:5-7 THE MESSAGE

FEBRUARY 14

As for me, O Lord, deal with me as your child, as one who bears your name!

PSALM 109:21 TLB

FEBRUARY 15

Everyone enjoys giving good advice,
and how wonderful it is to be able
to say the right thing at the right time!

PROVERBS 15:23 TLB

FEBRUARY 16

I am still confident of this: I will see
the goodness of the Lord in the land
of the living. Wait for the Lord; be strong
and take heart and wait for the Lord.

PSALM 27:13-14 NIV

FEBRUARY 17

My troubles turned out all for the best—
they forced me to learn from your textbook.
Truth from your mouth means more
to me than striking it rich in a gold mine.

PSALM 119:71-72 THE MESSAGE

FEBRUARY 18

The Lord reigns forever; he has established his throne for judgment. He will judge the world in righteousness; he will govern the peoples with justice.

PSALM 9:7-8 NIV

FEBRUARY 19

Blessed is the man who does not walk
in the counsel of the wicked or stand in the
way of sinners or sit in the seat of mockers.
But his delight is in the law of the Lord, and
on his law he meditates day and night.
He is like a tree planted by streams of water,
which yields its fruit in season and whose leaf
does not wither. Whatever he does prospers.

PSALM 1:1-3 NIV

FEBRUARY 20

Because you are my help,
I sing in the shadow of your wings.
My soul clings to you;
your right hand upholds me.

PSALM 63:7-8 NIV

FEBRUARY 21

In peace I will both lie down and sleep,
for You alone, O Lord,
make me to dwell in safety.

PSALM 4:8 NASB

FEBRUARY 22

Above all else, guard your heart,
for it is the wellspring of life…. Let your
eyes look straight ahead, fix your gaze
directly before you. Make level paths for
your feet and take only ways that are firm.

Proverbs 4:23,25-26 niv

February 23

May Your lovingkindnesses also
come to me, O Lord, Your salvation
according to Your word.

PSALM 119:41 NASB

FEBRUARY 24

Your word, O Lord, is eternal; it stands firm in the heavens. Your faithfulness continues through all generations; you established the earth, and it endures. Your laws endure to this day, for all things serve you.

PSALM 119:89-91 NIV

FEBRUARY 25

Be glad in the Lord and rejoice,
O righteous, and shout for joy,
all you upright in heart.

PSALM 32:11 NRSV

FEBRUARY 26

My soul faints with longing for your
salvation, but I have put my hope in your
word. My eyes fail, looking for your promise;
I say, "When will you comfort me?"...
Preserve my life according to your love,
and I will obey the statutes of your mouth.

PSALM 119:81-82,88 NIV

FEBRUARY 27

So, my dear friends, listen carefully;
those who embrace these my ways
are most blessed.

PROVERBS 8:32 THE MESSAGE

FEBRUARY 28

This is the gate of the Lord, through which the righteous shall enter. I will praise You, for You have answered me, and have become my salvation.... This is the day the Lord has made; we will rejoice and be glad in it.

PSALM 118:20-21,24 NKJV

FEBRUARY 29

Why are you cast down, O my soul,
and why are you disquieted within me?
Hope in God; for I shall again praise him,
my help and my God.

PSALM 43:5 NRSV

MARCH 1

You have made known to me the path of
life; you will fill me with joy in your presence,
with eternal pleasures at your right hand.

PSALM 16:11 NIV

MARCH 2

Let me understand the teaching
of your precepts; then I will meditate
on your wonders.

PSALM 119:27 NIV

MARCH 3

Know this: God is God, and God, God.
He made us; we didn't make him.
We're his people, his well-tended sheep….
For God is sheer beauty, all-generous in love,
loyal always and ever.

PSALM 100:3,5 THE MESSAGE

MARCH 4

There are "friends" who pretend
to be friends, but there is a friend
who sticks closer than a brother.

PROVERBS 18:24 TLB

MARCH 5

One thing I asked of the Lord, that will I seek after: to live in the house of the Lord all the days of my life, to behold the beauty of the Lord, and to inquire in his temple. For he will hide me in his shelter in the day of trouble; he will conceal me under the cover of his tent; he will set me high on a rock.

PSALM 27:4-5 NRSV

MARCH 6

How great is your goodness,
which you have stored up for those
who fear you, which you bestow in the sight
of men on those who take refuge in you.

PSALM 31:19 NIV

MARCH 7

He who keeps Israel will neither slumber
nor sleep. The Lord is your keeper;
the Lord is your shade at your right hand.

PSALM 121:4-5 NRSV

MARCH 8

Turn to me and have mercy on me,
as you always do to those who love your
name. Direct my footsteps according to your
word; let no sin rule over me. Redeem me
from the oppression of men, that I may obey
your precepts. Make your face shine upon
your servant and teach me your decrees.

PSALM 119:132-135 NIV

MARCH 9

$H$is love endures forever. To the One who remembered us in our low estate. His love endures forever. And freed us from our enemies, his love endures forever.

PSALM 136:22-24 NIV

MARCH 10

When a man's ways are pleasing
to the Lord, He makes even his enemies
to be at peace with him. Better is a little
with righteousness than great income
with injustice. The mind of man plans
his way, but the Lord directs his steps.

PROVERBS 16:7-9 NASB

MARCH 11

You hem me in—behind and before;
you have laid your hand upon me.
Such knowledge is too wonderful for me,
too lofty for me to attain.

PSALM 139:5-6 NIV

MARCH 12

Happy are those who do not follow
the advice of the wicked, or take the path that
sinners tread, or sit in the seat of scoffers;
but their delight is in the law of the Lord,
and on his law they meditate day and night.

PSALM 1:1-2 NRSV

MARCH 13

Skilled living gets its start in the Fear-of-
God, insight into life from knowing
a Holy God. It's through me, Lady Wisdom,
that your life deepens, and the years
of your life ripen. Live wisely and wisdom
will permeate your life.

PROVERBS 9:10-12 THE MESSAGE

MARCH 14

Some trust in chariots and some in horses,
but we trust in the name of the Lord our
God. They are brought to their knees and
fall, but we rise up and stand firm.

PSALM 20:7-8 NIV

MARCH 15

The heavens are telling the glory of God; they are a marvelous display of his craftsmanship. Day and night they keep on telling about God. Without a sound or word, silent in the skies, their message reaches out to all the world. The sun lives in the heavens where God placed it

PSALM 19:1-3 TLB

MARCH 16

Oh, how I love your law! I meditate
on it all day long. Your commands
make me wiser than my enemies,
for they are ever with me.

PSALM 119:97-98 NIV

MARCH 17

Let them shout for joy and be glad,
who favor my righteous cause; and let them
say continually, "Let the Lord be magnified,
who has pleasure in the prosperity of His
servant." And my tongue shall speak
of Your righteousness and of Your
praise all the day long.

PSALM 35:27-28 NKJV

MARCH 18

Even a child is known by his deeds,
whether what he does is pure and right.

PROVERBS 20:11 NKJV

MARCH 19

Praise the Lord, O my soul, and forget not
all his benefits...who redeems your life
from the pit and crowns you with love
and compassion, who satisfies your
desires with good things so that your
youth is renewed like the eagle's.

PSALM 103:2,4-5 NIV

MARCH 20

God made the heavens—
Royal splendor radiates from him,
a powerful beauty sets him apart.

PSALM 96:5-6 THE MESSAGE

MARCH 21

O Lord, You have searched me and known
me. You know when I sit down
and when I rise up; You understand
my thought from afar.

PSALM 139:1-2 NASB

MARCH 22

A glad heart makes a cheerful countenance,
but by sorrow of heart the spirit is broken....
All the days of the poor are hard,
but a cheerful heart has a continual feast.

PROVERBS 15:13,15 NRSV

MARCH 23

I will bless the Lord who counsels me;
he gives me wisdom in the night. He tells
me what to do. I am always thinking
of the Lord; and because he is so near,
I never need to stumble or to fall.
Heart, body, and soul are filled with joy.

PSALM 16:7-9 TLB

MARCH 24

Wait for the Lord, and keep His way,
and He will exalt you to inherit the land.

PSALM 37:34 NASB

MARCH 25

Hear my cry, O God; listen to my prayer.
From the ends of the earth I call to you,
I call as my heart grows faint;
lead me to the rock that is higher than I.
For you have been my refuge,
a strong tower against the foe.

PSALM 61:1-3 NIV

MARCH 26

Take note of how I love what you tell me;
out of your life of love, prolong my life.
Your words all add up to the sum total:
Truth. Your righteous decisions are eternal.

PSALM 119:159-160 THE MESSAGE

MARCH 27

A word aptly spoken is like apples of gold
in settings of silver. Like an earring of gold
or an ornament of fine gold is a wise
man's rebuke to a listening ear.

PROVERBS 25:11-12 NIV

MARCH 28

The steps of a man are established
by the Lord; and He delights in his way.
When he falls, he shall not be hurled
headlong; because the Lord
is the One who holds his hand.

PSALM 37:23-24 NASB

MARCH 29

Be still before the Lord and wait patiently
for him; do not fret when men succeed
in their ways, when they carry out their
wicked schemes. Refrain from anger and turn
from wrath; do not fret—it leads only to evil.

PSALM 37:7-8 NIV

MARCH 30

One thing God has spoken, two things
have I heard: that you, O God, are strong,
and that you, O Lord, are loving.
Surely you will reward each person
according to what he has done.

PSALM 62:11-12 NIV

MARCH 31

"Be still, and know that I am God;
I will be exalted among the nations,
I will be exalted in the earth."
The Lord Almighty is with us;
the God of Jacob is our fortress.

PSALM 46:10-11 NIV

APRIL 1

The law of the Lord is perfect, reviving
the soul. The statutes of the Lord are
trustworthy, making wise the simple.
The precepts of the Lord are right, giving
joy to the heart. The commands of the Lord
are radiant, giving light to the eyes. The fear
of the Lord is pure, enduring forever.
The ordinances of the Lord are sure
and altogether righteous.

PSALM 19:7-9 NIV

APRIL 2

The ways of right-living people glow
with light; the longer they live, the brighter
they shine…. Keep vigilant watch over
your heart; that's where life starts.

PROVERBS 4:18,23 THE MESSAGE

APRIL 3

Your statutes are my heritage forever;
they are the joy of my heart. My heart is set
on keeping your decrees to the very end.

PSALM 119:111-112 NIV

APRIL 4

Your kingdom is an everlasting kingdom,
and Your dominion endures throughout all
generations.... The eyes of all look to You,
and You give them their food in
due time. You open Your hand,
and satisfy the desire of every living thing.

PSALM 145:13,15-16 NASB

APRIL 5

Let them give thanks to the Lord for his
unfailing love…for he satisfies the thirsty
and fills the hungry with good things.

PSALM 107:8-9 NIV

APRIL 6

Y̶ou prepare a table before me
in the presence of my enemies;
you anoint my head with oil; my cup
overflows. Surely goodness and mercy
shall follow me all the days of my life,
and I shall dwell in the house
of the Lord my whole life long.

PSALM 23:5-6 NRSV

APRIL 7

The name of the Lord is a strong tower;
the righteous run to it and are safe.

PROVERBS 18:10 NIV

APRIL 8

As the deer pants for streams of water,
so my soul pants for you, O God. My soul
thirsts for God, for the living God. When can
I go and meet with God?... Put your hope
in God, for I will yet praise him, my Savior.

PSALM 42:1-2,5 NIV

APRIL 9

For you created my inmost being;
you knit me together in my mother's womb.
I praise you because I am fearfully
and wonderfully made; your works
are wonderful, I know that full well.

PSALM 139:13-14 NIV

APRIL 10

You've been a safe place for me,
a good place to hide…. I can always count
on you—God, my dependable love.

PSALM 59:16-17 THE MESSAGE

APRIL 11

Bless the Lord, O my soul. O Lord my God,
you are very great. You are clothed with
honor and majesty, wrapped in light as with
a garment. You stretch out the heavens like
a tent, you set the beams of your chambers
on the waters, you make the clouds your
chariot, you ride on the wings of the wind....
You set the earth on its foundations,
so that it shall never be shaken.

PSALM 104:1-3,5 NRSV

APRIL 12

Invigorate my soul so I can praise
you well, use your decrees to put iron
in my soul. And should I wander off
like a lost sheep—seek me! I'll recognize
the sound of your voice.

PSALM 119:175-176 THE MESSAGE

APRIL 13

The Lord is my rock and my fortress
and my deliverer, my God, my rock,
in whom I take refuge; my shield
and the horn of my salvation,
my stronghold.

PSALM 18:2 NASB

APRIL 14

For all God's words are right, and everything
he does is worthy of our trust. He loves
whatever is just and good; the earth is filled
with his tender love. He merely spoke,
and the heavens were formed, and all
the galaxies of stars. He made the oceans,
pouring them into his vast reservoirs.

PSALM 33:4-7 TLB

APRIL 15

In the fear of the Lord one has strong
confidence, and one's children
will have a refuge.

PROVERBS 14:26 NRSV

APRIL 16

The Lord is righteous in all his ways
and loving toward all he has made.
The Lord is near to all who call on him,
to all who call on him in truth. He fulfills
the desires of those who fear him;
he hears their cry and saves them.

PSALM 145:17-19 NIV

APRIL 17

Sustain me according to your promise,
and I will live; do not let my hopes be
dashed. Uphold me, and I will be delivered;
I will always have regard for your decrees.

PSALM 119:116-117 NIV

APRIL 18

Our mouths were filled with laughter, our tongues with songs of joy. Then it was said among the nations, "The Lord has done great things for them." The Lord has done great things for us, and we are filled with joy.

PSALM 126:1-3 NIV

APRIL 19

Ascribe to the Lord the glory due his name;
worship the Lord in the splendor of his
holiness. The voice of the Lord is over
the waters; the God of glory thunders,
the Lord thunders over the mighty waters.
The voice of the Lord is powerful;
the voice of the Lord is majestic.

PSALM 29:2-4 NIV

APRIL 20

You know me inside and out…You know
exactly how I was made, bit by bit,
how I was sculpted from nothing into
something. Like an open book, you watched
me grow from conception to birth;
all the stages of my life were spread out
before you…before I'd even lived one day.

PSALM 139:15-16 THE MESSAGE

APRIL 21

Let love and faithfulness never leave you;
bind them around your neck, write them
on the tablet of your heart.

PROVERBS 3:3 NIV

APRIL 22

Look upon my suffering and deliver me,
for I have not forgotten your law.
Defend my cause and redeem me;
preserve my life according to your promise.

PSALM 119:153-154 NIV

APRIL 23

Oh come, let us worship and bow down;
let us kneel before the Lord our Maker.
For He is our God, and we are the people
of His pasture, and the sheep of His hand.

PSALM 95:6-7 NKJV

APRIL 24

We wait in hope for the Lord; he is our help and our shield. In him our hearts rejoice, for we trust in his holy name. May your unfailing love rest upon us, O Lord, even as we put our hope in you.

PSALM 33:20-22 NIV

APRIL 25

For his anger is but for a moment;
his favor is for a lifetime. Weeping
may linger for the night, but joy
comes with the morning.

PSALM 30:5 NRSV

APRIL 26

Create in me a pure heart, O God,
and renew a steadfast spirit within me....
The sacrifices of God are a broken spirit;
a broken and contrite heart, O God,
you will not despise.

PSALM 51:10,17 NIV

APRIL 27

Great peace have they who love your law,
and nothing can make them stumble. I wait
for your salvation, O Lord, and I follow your
commands. I obey your statutes, for I love
them greatly. I obey your precepts and your
statutes, for all my ways are known to you.

PSALM 119:165-168 NIV

APRIL 28

A wise person gets known for insight;
gracious words add to one's reputation.

PROVERBS 16:21 THE MESSAGE

APRIL 29

I cry aloud to the Lord; I lift up my voice to the Lord for mercy…. When my spirit grows faint within me, it is you who know my way. In the path where I walk men have hidden a snare for me.

PSALM 142:1,3 NIV

APRIL 30

The Lord is gracious and full of
compassion, slow to anger and
great in mercy.

PSALM 145:8 NKJV

MAY 1

Delight yourself in the Lord and he will give you the desires of your heart. Commit your way to the Lord; trust in him and he will do this: He will make your righteousness shine like the dawn, the justice of your cause like the noonday sun.

PSALM 37:4-6 NIV

MAY 2

Cling to wisdom—she will protect you.
Love her—she will guard you. Getting
wisdom is the most important thing
you can do! And with your wisdom,
develop common sense and good judgment.

PROVERBS 4:6-7 TLB

MAY 3

Trouble and distress have come upon me,
but your commands are my delight.
Your statutes are forever right;
give me understanding that I may live.

PSALM 119:143-144 NIV

MAY 4

Even the sparrow has found a home,
and the swallow a nest for herself,
where she may have her young—a place
near your altar, O Lord Almighty, my King
and my God. Blessed are those who dwell
in your house; they are ever praising you.

PSALM 84:3-4 NIV

MAY 5

H umility and reverence for the Lord
will make you both wise and honored.

PROVERBS 15:33 TLB

MAY 6

You own the day, you own the night;
you put stars and sun in place. You laid out
the four corners of earth, shaped
the seasons of summer and winter.

PSALM 74:16-17 THE MESSAGE

MAY 7

Deep calls to deep in the roar of your
waterfalls; all your waves and breakers
have swept over me. By day the Lord directs
his love, at night his song is with me—
a prayer to the God of my life.

PSALM 42:7-8 NIV

MAY 8

He will cover you with his feathers,
and under his wings you will find refuge;
his faithfulness will be your shield
and rampart. You will not fear the terror
of night, nor the arrow that flies by day.

PSALM 91:4-5 NIV

MAY 9

The earth is the Lord's, and everything
in it, the world, and all who live in it;
for he founded it upon the seas
and established it upon the waters.

PSALM 24:1-2 NIV

MAY 10

Praise the Lord! Praise, O servants
of the Lord, Praise the name of the Lord!
Blessed be the name of the Lord from
this time forth and forevermore! From
the rising of the sun to its going down
the Lord's name is to be praised.

PSALM 113:1-3 NKJV

MAY 11

I rise before dawn and cry for help;
I have put my hope in your word.
My eyes stay open through the watches
of the night, that I may meditate on your
promises. Hear my voice in accordance
with your love; preserve my life,
O Lord, according to your laws.

PSALM 119:147-149 NIV

MAY 12

By wisdom a house is built, and through understanding it is established.

PROVERBS 24:3 NIV

MAY 13

Bless the Lord, O my soul; and all that
is within me, bless His holy name!
Bless the Lord, O my soul, and forget not all
His benefits: who forgives all your iniquities,
who heals all your diseases.

PSALM 103:1-3 NKJV

MAY 14

But I will always trust in you
and in your mercy and shall rejoice
in your salvation. I will sing to the Lord
because he has blessed me so richly.

PSALM 13:5-6 TLB

MAY 15

The boundary lines have fallen for me
in pleasant places; surely I have a delightful
inheritance. I will praise the Lord,
who counsels me; even at night
my heart instructs me. I have set
the Lord always before me. Because he
is at my right hand, I will not be shaken.

PSALM 16:6-8 NIV

MAY 16

Pleasant words are a honeycomb,
sweet to the soul and healing to the bones.

PROVERBS 16:24 NIV

MAY 17

Let my cry come right into your presence,
God; provide me with the insight that comes
only from your Word. Give my request
your personal attention, rescue me
on the terms of your promise.

PSALM 119:169-170 THE MESSAGE

MAY 18

Where can I go from your Spirit?
Where can I flee from your presence?
If I go up to the heavens, you are there;
if I make my bed in the depths, you are there.
If I rise on the wings of the dawn,
if I settle on the far side of the sea,
even there your hand will guide me,
your right hand will hold me fast.

PSALM 139:7-10 NIV

MAY 19

Let another praise you, and not your own
mouth; someone else, and not your own lips.

May 20

Blessed is the nation whose God is the Lord,
the people he chose for his inheritance.
From heaven the Lord looks down and sees
all mankind; from his dwelling place he
watches all who live on earth—he who forms
the hearts of all, who considers everything
they do…. But the eyes of the Lord are
on those who fear him, on those whose
hope is in his unfailing love.

PSALM 33:12-15,18 NIV

MAY 21

I bless God every chance I get; my lungs expand with his praise. I live and breathe God; if things aren't going well, hear this and be happy: Join me in spreading the news; together let's get the word out.

PSALM 34:1-3 THE MESSAGE

MAY 22

Lift up your heads, O you gates; lift them up, you ancient doors, that the King of glory may come in. Who is he, this King of glory? The Lord Almighty—he is the King of glory.

PSALM 24:9-10 NIV

MAY 23

The Lord is my light and my salvation—
whom shall I fear? The Lord is the stronghold
of my life—of whom shall I be afraid?...
Hear my voice when I call, O Lord;
be merciful to me and answer me.
My heart says of you, "Seek his face!"
Your face, Lord, I will seek.

PSALM 27:1,7-8 NIV

MAY 24

Knowing what is right is like deep
water in the heart; a wise person draws
from the well within.

PROVERBS 20:5 THE MESSAGE

MAY 25

Your promises have been thoroughly
tested, and your servant loves them....
Your righteousness is everlasting
and your law is true.

PSALM 119:140,142 NIV

MAY 26

I will exalt you, O Lord, for you lifted
me out of the depths and did not let my
enemies gloat over me. O Lord my God,
I called to you for help and you healed me.
O Lord, you brought me up from the grave;
you spared me from going down into
the pit. Sing to the Lord, you saints of his;
praise his holy name.

PSALM 30:1-4 NIV

MAY 27

Test me, O Lord, and try me, examine
my heart and my mind; for your love
is ever before me, and I walk
continually in your truth.

PSALM 26:2-3 NIV

MAY 28

Let us see your miracles again; let our
children see glorious things, the kind you
used to do, and let the Lord our God favor
us and give us success. May he give
permanence to all we do.

PSALM 90:16-17 TLB

MAY 29

All the creatures look expectantly to you
to give them their meals on time. You come,
and they gather around; you open your hand
and they eat from it.... Send out your Spirit
and they spring to life—the whole
countryside in bloom and blossom.

PSALM 104:27,30 THE MESSAGE

MAY 30

Do not withhold good from those who
deserve it, when it is in your power to act.

PROVERBS 3:27 NIV

MAY 31

When I consider your heavens, the work
of your fingers, the moon and the stars,
which you have set in place, what is man
that you are mindful of him, the son of man
that you care for him? You made him
a little lower than the heavenly beings
and crowned him with glory and honor.

PSALM 8:3-5 NIV

JUNE 1

God is our refuge and strength, a very present help in trouble. Therefore we will not fear, though the earth should change, though the mountains shake in the heart of the sea.

PSALM 46:1-2 NRSV

JUNE 2

Who is God besides the Lord? And who is the Rock except our God? It is God who arms me with strength and makes my way perfect. He makes my feet like the feet of a deer; he enables me to stand on the heights.

PSALM 18:31-33 NIV

JUNE 3

Your statutes are wonderful; therefore
I obey them. The unfolding of your
words gives light; it gives understanding
to the simple. I open my mouth and pant,
longing for your commands.

PSALM 119:129-131 NIV

JUNE 4

May the Lord answer you when you are
in distress; may the name of the God of Jacob
protect you. May he send you help from
the sanctuary and grant you support from
Zion…. May he give you the desire of your
heart and make all your plans succeed.
We will shout for joy when you are
victorious and will lift up our
banners in the name of our God.
May the Lord grant all your requests.

PSALM 20:1-2,4-5 NIV

JUNE 5

A cheerful look brings joy to the heart,
and good news gives health to the bones.

PROVERBS 15:30 NIV

JUNE 6

In you, O Lord, I have taken refuge;
let me never be put to shame; deliver me
in your righteousness. Turn your ear to me,
come quickly to my rescue; be my rock
of refuge, a strong fortress to save me.
Since you are my rock and my fortress,
for the sake of your name lead and guide
me…. Into your hands I commit my spirit;
redeem me, O Lord, the God of truth.

PSALM 31:1-5 NIV

JUNE 7

Guard my life and rescue me; let me not
be put to shame, for I take refuge in you.
May integrity and uprightness protect me,
because my hope is in you.

PSALM 25:20-21 NIV

JUNE 8

Have mercy on me, O God…. Wash away
all my iniquity and cleanse me from my
sin…. Surely you desire truth in the
inner parts; you teach me wisdom
in the inmost place.

PSALM 51:1-2,6 NIV

JUNE 9

By your words I can see where I'm going;
they throw a beam of light on my dark path.
I've committed myself and I'll never turn
back from living by your righteous order.

PSALM 119:105-106 THE MESSAGE

JUNE 10

Cast your cares on the Lord and he will
sustain you; he will never let the
righteous fall…. As for me, I trust in you.

PSALM 55:22-23 NIV

JUNE 11

My son, do not despise the Lord's
discipline and do not resent his rebuke,
because the Lord disciplines those he loves,
as a father the son he delights in.

PROVERBS 3:11-12 NIV

JUNE 12

You answer us with awesome deeds
of righteousness, O God our Savior, the hope
of all the ends of the earth and of the farthest
seas, who formed the mountains by your
power, having armed yourself with strength,
who stilled the roaring of the seas, the roaring of their waves, and the turmoil of the
nations. Those living far away fear your wonders; where morning dawns and evening
fades you call forth songs of joy.

PSALM 65:5-8 NIV

JUNE 13

I'm thanking you, God, out in the streets,
singing your praises in town and country.
The deeper your love, the higher it goes;
every cloud's a flag to your faithfulness.
Soar high in the skies, O God! Cover
the whole earth with your glory!

PSALM 108:3-5 THE MESSAGE

JUNE 14

For you have been my hope, O Sovereign Lord, my confidence since my youth. From birth I have relied on you; you brought me forth from my mother's womb. I will ever praise you…. My mouth is filled with your praise, declaring your splendor all day long.

PSALM 70:5-6,8 NIV

JUNE 15

Praise be to the Lord God, the God of Israel,
who alone does marvelous deeds.
Praise be to his glorious name forever;
may the whole earth be filled with his glory.
Amen and Amen.

PSALM 72:18-19 NIV

JUNE 16

As for me, it is good to be near God.
I have made the Sovereign Lord my refuge;
I will tell of all your deeds.

PSALM 73:28 NIV

JUNE 17

Let your hand rest on the man at your right hand, the son of man you have raised up for yourself. Then we will not turn away from you; revive us, and we will call on your name. Restore us, O God; make your face shine upon us, that we may be saved.

PSALM 80:17-19 NIV

JUNE 18

As water reflects a face,
so a man's heart reflects the man.

PROVERBS 27:19 NIV

JUNE 19

Love and faithfulness meet together;
righteousness and peace kiss each other.
Faithfulness springs forth from the earth,
and righteousness looks down from heaven.
The Lord will indeed give what is good,
and our land will yield its harvest.
Righteousness goes before him
and prepares the way for his steps.

PSALM 85:10-13 NIV

JUNE 20

Righteous are you, O Lord, and your laws
are right. The statutes you have laid down
are righteous; they are fully trustworthy.

PSALM 119:137-138 NIV

JUNE 21

The righteous will flourish like a palm tree,
they will grow like a cedar of Lebanon;
planted in the house of the Lord,
they will flourish in the courts of our God.
They will still bear fruit in old age,
they will stay fresh and green, proclaiming,
"The Lord is upright; he is my Rock,
and there is no wickedness in him."

PSALM 92:12-15 NIV

JUNE 22

Get out the message—God Rules!
He put the world on a firm foundation;
    He treats everyone fair and square.
Let's hear it from Sky, with Earth joining in,
and a huge round of applause from Sea.

PSALM 96:10-11 THE MESSAGE

JUNE 23

Let the sea resound, and everything in it,
the world, and all who live in it. Let the rivers
clap their hands, let the mountains sing
together for joy; let them sing before
the Lord, for he comes to judge the earth.

PSALM 98:7-9 NIV

JUNE 24

Fire goes before [the Lord] and consumes his foes on every side. His lightning lights up the world; the earth sees and trembles. The mountains melt like wax before the Lord, before the Lord of all the earth. The heavens proclaim his righteousness, and all the peoples see his glory.

PSALM 97:3-6 NIV

JUNE 25

The King is mighty, he loves justice—
you have established equity; in Jacob
you have done what is just and right.
Exalt the Lord our God and worship
at his footstool; he is holy.

PSALM 99:4-5 NIV

JUNE 26

Oh, love me—and right now!—
hold me tight! just the way you promised.
Now comfort me so I can live, really live;
your revelation is the tune I dance to.

PSALM 119:76-77 THE MESSAGE

JUNE 27

My heart is steadfast, O God; I will sing
and make music with all my soul. Awake,
harp and lyre! I will awaken the dawn.
I will praise you, O Lord, among the nations;
I will sing of you among the peoples.

PSALM 108:1-3 NIV

JUNE 28

Just as iron sharpens iron,
a friend sharpens a friend.

PROVERBS 27:17 NLT

JUNE 29

The Lord is exalted over all the nations, his glory above the heavens. Who is like the Lord our God, the One who sits enthroned on high, who stoops down to look on the heavens and the earth?

PSALM 113:4-6 NIV

JUNE 30

Hallelujah! Blessed man, blessed woman, who fear God, who cherish and relish his commandments, their children robust on the earth, and the homes of the upright—how blessed!

PSALM 112:1-2 THE MESSAGE

JULY 1

Though the Lord is on high, he looks upon
the lowly, but the proud he knows from afar.
Though I walk in the midst of trouble,
you preserve my life; you stretch out your
hand against the anger of my foes,
with your right hand you save me.
The Lord will fulfill his purpose for me;
your love, O Lord, endures forever—
do not abandon the works of your hands.

PSALM 138:6-8 NIV

JULY 2

Show me your ways, O Lord, teach me your
paths; guide me in your truth and teach me,
for you are God my Savior, and my hope
is in you all day long.

PSALM 25:4-5 NIV

JULY 3

Mvay the peoples praise you, O God;
may all the peoples praise you.
May the nations be glad and sing for joy,
for you rule the peoples justly and guide
the nations of the earth.

PSALM 67:3-4 NIV

JULY 4

But there is forgiveness with You,
that You may be feared. I wait for
the Lord, my soul does wait, and in His word
do I hope. My soul waits for the Lord more
than the watchmen for the morning; indeed,
more than the watchmen for the morning.

PSALM 130:4-6 NASB

JULY 5

I love those who love me, and those who seek me diligently will find me.

PROVERBS 8:17 NKJV

JULY 6

Those who trust in the Lord are like Mount
Zion, which cannot be shaken but endures
forever. As the mountains surround
Jerusalem, so the Lord surrounds his people
both now and forevermore.

PSALM 125:1-2 NIV

JULY 7

Therefore let everyone who is godly pray
to you while you may be found; surely when
the mighty waters rise, they will not reach
him. You are my hiding place; you will
protect me from trouble and surround
me with songs of deliverance.

PSALM 32:6-7 NIV

JULY 8

Know also that wisdom is sweet to your soul; if you find it, there is a future hope for you, and your hope will not be cut off.

PROVERBS 24:14 NIV

JULY 9

The Lord is my shepherd; I shall not want.
He makes me to lie down in green pastures;
He leads me beside the still waters.

PSALM 23:1-2 NKJV

JULY 10

Give ear to my words, O Lord, consider
my sighing. Listen to my cry for help,
my King and my God, for to you I pray.
In the morning, O Lord, you hear my voice;
in the morning I lay my requests before
you and wait in expectation.

PSALM 5:1-3 NIV

JULY 11

I will lift up my eyes to the mountains;
from where shall my help come?
My help comes from the Lord,
who made heaven and earth.

PSALM 121:1-2 NASB

JULY 12

Let the wise listen and add to their learning,
and let the discerning get guidance....
The fear of the Lord is the beginning
of knowledge, but fools despise
wisdom and discipline.

PROVERBS 1:5,7 NIV

JULY 13

But You, O Lord, are a shield about me,
my glory, and the One who lifts my head.
I was crying to the Lord with my voice,
and He answered me from His holy
mountain. I lay down and slept; I awoke,
for the Lord sustains me.

PSALM 3:3-5 NASB

JULY 14

Answer me when I call to you,
O my righteous God. Give me relief
from my distress; be merciful to me
and hear my prayer.

PSALM 4:1 NIV

JULY 15

May the Lord continually bless you with
heaven's blessings as well as with human joys.

PSALM 128:5 TLB

JULY 16

Gracious is the Lord, and righteous;
our God is merciful. The Lord protects
the simple; when I was brought low,
he saved me. Return, O my soul, to your rest,
for the Lord has dealt bountifully with you.

PSALM 116:5-7 NRSV

JULY 17

A cheerful heart is good medicine,
but a crushed spirit dries up the bones.

PROVERBS 17:22 NIV

JULY 18

With your very own hands you formed me;
now breathe your wisdom over me so I can
understand you. When they see me waiting,
expecting your Word, those who fear you will
take heart and be glad. I can see now, God,
that your decisions are right; your testing
has taught me what's true and right.

PSALM 119:73-75 THE MESSAGE

JULY 19

But I pray to you, O Lord, in the time
of your favor; in your great love, O God,
answer me with your sure salvation.

PSALM 69:13 NIV

JULY 20

For the Lord God is a sun and shield;
the Lord bestows favor and honor;
no good thing does he withhold from those
whose walk is blameless. O Lord Almighty,
blessed is the man who trusts in you.

PSALM 84:11-12 NIV

JULY 21

Answer me quickly, O Lord; my spirit fails.
Do not hide your face from me, or I shall be
like those who go down to the Pit. Let me
hear of your steadfast love in the morning,
for in you I put my trust. Teach me the way
I should go, for to you I lift up my soul.

PSALM 143:7-8 NRSV

JULY 22

You are my God, and I will praise You;
You are my God, I will exalt You. Oh,
give thanks to the Lord, for He is good!
For His mercy endures forever.

PSALM 118:28-29 NKJV

JULY 23

Hear, my child, your father's instruction,
and do not reject your mother's teaching;
for they are a fair garland for your head,
and pendants for your neck.

PROVERBS 1:8-9 NRSV

JULY 24

Not unto us, O Lord, not unto us, but to Your name give glory, because of Your mercy, because of Your truth.

PSALM 115:1 NKJV

JULY 25

As a father has compassion on his children,
so the Lord has compassion on those who
fear him; for he knows how we are formed,
he remembers that we are dust.
As for man, his days are like grass,
he flourishes like a flower of the field.

PSALM 103:13-15 NIV

JULY 26

Then I lay down and slept in peace and woke up safely, for the Lord was watching over me. And now, although ten thousand enemies surround me on every side, I am not afraid.

PSALM 3:5-6 TLB

JULY 27

My shield is God Most High, who saves
the upright in heart. God is a righteous
judge…. I will give thanks to the Lord
because of his righteousness and will sing
praise to the name of the Lord Most High.

Psalm 7:10-11,17 niv

July 28

May the words of my mouth
and the meditation of my heart be pleasing
in your sight, O Lord, my Rock
and my Redeemer.

PSALM 19:14 NIV

JULY 29

You need not be afraid of disaster
or the plots of wicked men, for the Lord
is with you; he protects you.

PROVERBS 3:24 TLB

JULY 30

He restores my soul. He guides me in paths
of righteousness for his name's sake.
Even though I walk through the valley
of the shadow of death, I will fear no evil,
for you are with me; your rod and your staff,
they comfort me.

PSALM 23:3-4 NIV

JULY 31

The ordinances of the Lord are sure and altogether righteous. They are more precious than gold, than much pure gold; they are sweeter than honey, than honey from the comb. By them is your servant warned; in keeping them there is great reward.

PSALM 19:9-11 NIV

AUGUST 1

Praise the Lord from the earth, you great sea
creatures and all ocean depths, lightning
and hail, snow and clouds, stormy winds
that do his bidding…small creatures
and flying birds, kings of the earth
and all nations, you princes and all rulers
on earth, young men and maidens, old men
and children. Let them praise the name
of the Lord, for his name alone is exalted.

PSALM 148:7-13 NIV

AUGUST 2

Trust in the Lord with all your heart
and lean not on your own understanding;
in all your ways acknowledge him,
and he will make your paths straight.

PROVERBS 3:5-6 NIV

AUGUST 3

I will hasten and not delay to obey your commands.... At midnight I rise to give you thanks for your righteous laws. I am a friend to all who fear you, to all who follow your precepts. The earth is filled with your love, O Lord; teach me your decrees.

PSALM 119:60-64 NIV

AUGUST 4

Praise God in his sanctuary; praise him
in his mighty heavens. Praise him
for his acts of power; praise him
for his surpassing greatness.

Psalm 150:1-2 niv

August 5

My child, if you accept my words
and treasure up my commandments within
you, making your ear attentive to wisdom
and inclining your heart to understanding;
if you indeed cry out for insight, and raise
your voice for understanding; if you seek
it like silver, and search for it as for hidden
treasures—then you will understand the fear
of the Lord and find the knowledge of God.

PROVERBS 2:1-5 NRSV

AUGUST 6

For you, O Lord, have delivered my soul
from death, my eyes from tears, my feet from
stumbling, that I may walk before the Lord
in the land of the living.

PSALM 116:8-9 NIV

AUGUST 7

He paid the ransom for his people,
He ordered his Covenant kept forever.
He's so personal and holy, worthy of our
respect. The good life begins in the fear
of God—do that and you'll know the blessing
of God. His Hallelujah lasts forever!

PSALM 111:9-10 THE MESSAGE

AUGUST 8

Praise the Lord from the heavens, praise him in the heights above. Praise him, all his angels, praise him, all his heavenly hosts. Praise him, sun and moon, praise him, all you shining stars. Praise him, you highest heavens and you waters above the skies. Let them praise the name of the Lord, for he commanded and they were created.

PSALM 148:1-5 NIV

AUGUST 9

He is the Lord our God; his judgments are in all the earth. He remembers his covenant forever, the word he commanded, for a thousand generations.

PSALM 105:7-8 NIV

AUGUST 10

The one who blesses others is abundantly blessed; those who help others are helped.

AUGUST 11

The Lord reigns, let the nations tremble;
he sits enthroned between the cherubim,
let the earth shake. Great is the Lord in Zion;
he is exalted over all the nations.
Let them praise your great
and awesome name—he is holy.

PSALM 99:1-3

AUGUST 12

I will sing to the Lord all my life;
I will sing praise to my God as long as I live.
May my meditation be pleasing to him,
as I rejoice in the Lord.

PSALM 104:33-34 NIV

AUGUST 13

The nations will fear the name
of the Lord, all the kings
of the earth will revere your glory.

PSALM 102:15 NIV

AUGUST 14

My theme song is God's love and justice,
and I'm singing it right to you, God.
I'm finding my way down the road of right
living, but how long before you show up?
I'm doing the very best I can, and I'm doing
it at home, where it counts.

PSALM 101:1-2 THE MESSAGE

AUGUST 15

Restore us again, O God our Savior,
and put away your displeasure toward us….
Show us your unfailing love, O Lord,
and grant us your salvation.

PSALM 85:4,7 NIV

AUGUST 16

Righteousness and justice are the foundation of your throne; love and faithfulness go before you. Blessed are those who have learned to acclaim you, who walk in the light of your presence, O Lord. They rejoice in your name all day long; they exult in your righteousness. For you are their glory and strength.

PSALM 89:14-17 NIV

AUGUST 17

Your statutes stand firm; holiness adorns
your house for endless days, O Lord.

PSALM 93:5 NIV

AUGUST 18

For the Lord gives wisdom, and from his
mouth come knowledge and understanding.
He holds victory in store for the upright,
he is a shield to those whose walk
is blameless, for he guards the course
of the just and protects the way
of his faithful ones.

PROVERBS 2:6-8 NIV

AUGUST 19

Remember your word to your servant,
for you have given me hope.
My comfort in my suffering is this:
Your promise preserves my life.

PSALM 119:49-50 NIV

AUGUST 20

Sing to God, O kingdoms of the earth,
sing praise to the Lord, to him who rides
the ancient skies above, who thunders
with mighty voice. Proclaim the power
of God...whose power is in the skies.
You are awesome, O God, in your sanctuary;
the God of Israel gives power and strength
to his people. Praise be to God!

PSALM 68:32-35 NIV

AUGUST 21

O God, you are my God, earnestly
I seek you; my soul thirsts for you,
my body longs for you, in a dry and weary
land where there is no water.

PSALM 63:1 NIV

AUGUST 22

Come and listen, all you who fear God;
let me tell you what he has done for me.
I cried out to him with my mouth; his praise
was on my tongue. If I had cherished sin in
my heart, the Lord would not have listened;
but God has surely listened and heard
my voice in prayer. Praise be to God,
who has not rejected my prayer or withheld
his love from me!

PSALM 66:16-20 NIV

AUGUST 23

There is a river whose streams make glad the city of God, the holy place where the Most High dwells. God is within her, she will not fall; God will help her at break of day. Nations are in uproar, kingdoms fall; he lifts his voice, the earth melts. The Lord Almighty is with us.

PSALM 46:4-6 NIV

AUGUST 24

Charm can mislead and beauty soon fades.
The woman to be admired and praised
is the woman who lives in the Fear-of-God.

PROVERBS 31:30 THE MESSAGE

AUGUST 25

Blessed is the man who makes the Lord his
trust, who does not look to the proud,
to those who turn aside to false gods. Many,
O Lord my God, are the wonders you have
done. The things you planned for us no one
can recount to you; were I to speak and tell
of them, they would be too many to declare.

PSALM 40:4-5 NIV

AUGUST 26

I wait for you, O Lord; you will answer,
O Lord my God…. O Lord, do not forsake
me; be not far from me, O my God.
Come quickly to help me, O Lord my Savior.

PSALM 38:15,21-22 NIV

AUGUST 27

The Lord loves the just and will not forsake his faithful ones. They will be protected forever, but the offspring of the wicked will be cut off; the righteous will inherit the land and dwell in it forever. The mouth of the righteous man utters wisdom, and his tongue speaks what is just. The law of his God is in his heart; his feet do not slip.

PSALM 37:28-31 NIV

AUGUST 28

I will praise you among the nations,
O Lord; I will sing praises to your name.
He gives his king great victories; he shows
unfailing kindness to his anointed.

PSALM 18:49-50 NIV

AUGUST 29

For the Lord gives wisdom, and from
his mouth come knowledge
and understanding…. Then you will
understand what is right and just and fair—
every good path. For wisdom will enter
your heart, and knowledge will be pleasant
to your soul. Discretion will protect you,
and understanding will guard you.

PROVERBS 2:6,9-11 NIV

AUGUST 30

Love the Lord, all his saints! The Lord
preserves the faithful, but the proud he pays
back in full. Be strong and take heart,
all you who hope in the Lord.

PSALM 31:22-24 NIV

AUGUST 31

Direct me in the path of your commands,
for there I find delight. Turn my heart toward
your statutes and not toward selfish gain.
Turn my eyes away from worthless things;
preserve my life according to your word.

PSALM 119:35-37 NIV

SEPTEMBER 1

I love the Lord because he hears my prayers and answers them. Because he bends down and listens, I will pray as long as I breathe!

PSALM 116:1-2 TLB

SEPTEMBER 2

Come, my children, listen to me; I will teach you the fear of the Lord. Whoever of you loves life and desires to see many good days, keep your tongue from evil and your lips from speaking lies. Turn from evil and do good; seek peace and pursue it.

PSALM 34:11-14 NIV

SEPTEMBER 3

Do not withhold Your tender mercies
from me, O Lord; let Your lovingkindness
and Your truth continually preserve me.

PSALM 40:11 NKJV

SEPTEMBER 4

He who conceals his sins does not prosper,
but whoever confesses and renounces
them finds mercy.

PROVERBS 28:13 NIV

SEPTEMBER 5

I waited patiently for the Lord; he turned to me and heard my cry. He lifted me out of the slimy pit, out of the mud and mire; he set my feet on a rock and gave me a firm place to stand. He put a new song in my mouth, a hymn of praise to our God. Many will see and fear and put their trust in the Lord.

PSALM 40:1-3 NIV

SEPTEMBER 6

Clap your hands, all you nations;
shout to God with cries of joy.
How awesome is the Lord Most High,
the great King over all the earth!

PSALM 47:1-2 NIV

SEPTEMBER 7

This God—his way is perfect; the promise
of the Lord proves true; he is a shield
for all who take refuge in him.

PSALM 18:30 NRSV

SEPTEMBER 8

Send forth your light and your truth,
let them guide me; let them bring me to your
holy mountain, to the place where you dwell.
Then will I go to the altar of God, to God,
my joy and my delight. I will praise you
with the harp, O God, my God.

PSALM 43:3-4 NIV

SEPTEMBER 9

My child, do not forget my teaching,
but let your heart keep my commandments;
for length of days and years of life
and abundant welfare they will give you.

Proverbs 3:1-2 NRSV

September 10

O Lord, you will hear the desire
of the meek; you will strengthen their heart,
you will incline your ear to do justice
for the orphan and the oppressed, so that
those from earth may strike terror no more.

PSALM 10:17-18 NRSV

SEPTEMBER 11

All mankind will fear; they will proclaim
the works of God and ponder what he
has done. Let the righteous rejoice
in the Lord and take refuge in him;
let all the upright in heart praise him!

PSALM 64:9-10 NIV

SEPTEMBER 12

Search me, O God, and know my heart;
test me and know my anxious thoughts.
See if there is any offensive way in me,
and lead me in the way everlasting.

PSALM 139:23-24 NIV

SEPTEMBER 13

Affirm your promises to me—promises
made to all who fear you. Deflect the harsh
words of my critics—but what you say
is always so good. See how hungry I am
for your counsel; preserve my life through
your righteous ways!

Psalm 119:38-40 the message

September 14

A friend loves at all times.

PROVERBS 17:17 NKJV

SEPTEMBER 15

You care for the land and water it; you
enrich it abundantly. The streams of God
are filled with water to provide the people
with grain, for so you have ordained it.
You drench its furrows and level its ridges;
you soften it with showers and bless its crops.
You crown the year with your bounty,
and your carts overflow with abundance.

PSALM 65:9-11 NIV

SEPTEMBER 16

Praise be to the Lord, to God our Savior,
who daily bears our burdens.
Our God is a God who saves.

PSALM 68:19-20 NIV

SEPTEMBER 17

For you, O Lord, have made me glad
by your work; at the works of your hands
I sing for joy. How great are your works,
O Lord! Your thoughts are very deep!

PSALM 92:4-5 NRSV

SEPTEMBER 18

Come and see what God has done, how
awesome his works in man's behalf!
He turned the sea into dry land, they passed
through the waters on foot—come, let us
rejoice in him. He rules forever by his power,
his eyes watch the nations—let not
the rebellious rise up against him.

PSALM 66:5-7 NIV

SEPTEMBER 19

Do not be wise in your own eyes;
fear the Lord and shun evil.
This will bring health to your body
and nourishment to your bones.

PROVERBS 3:7-8 NIV

SEPTEMBER 20

Bend an ear, God; answer me. I'm one
miserable wretch! Keep me safe—haven't
I lived a good life? Help your servant—
I'm depending on you! You're my God;
have mercy on me. I count on you
from morning to night.

PSALM 86:1-3 THE MESSAGE

SEPTEMBER 21

When I said, "My foot is slipping,"
your love, O Lord, supported me.
When anxiety was great within me,
your consolation brought joy to my soul.

PSALM 94:18-19 NIV

SEPTEMBER 22

For the Lord is the great God, the great King above all gods. In his hand are the depths of the earth, and the mountain peaks belong to him. The sea is his, for he made it, and his hands formed the dry land.

PSALM 95:3-5 NIV

SEPTEMBER 23

With my lips I recount all the laws that
come from your mouth. I rejoice in following
your statutes as one rejoices in great riches.
I meditate on your precepts and consider
your ways. I delight in your decrees;
I will not neglect your word.

PSALM 119:13-16 NIV

SEPTEMBER 24

H e who pursues righteousness
and love finds life, prosperity and honor.

PROVERBS 21:21 NIV

SEPTEMBER 25

All the ends of the earth have seen
the salvation of our God. Shout for joy
to the Lord, all the earth, burst into jubilant
song with music; make music to the Lord
with the harp, with the harp and the sound
of singing, with trumpets and the blast
of the ram's horn—shout for joy before
the Lord, the King.

PSALM 98:3-6 NIV

SEPTEMBER 26

But you, O Lord, are enthroned forever;
your name endures to all generations.
You will rise up and have compassion
on Zion, for it is time to favor it;
the appointed time has come.

PSALM 102:12-13 NRSV

SEPTEMBER 27

His miracles are his memorial—this God of Grace, this God of Love. He gave food to those who fear him, He remembered to keep his ancient promise. He proved to his people that he could do what he said: Hand them the nations on a platter—a gift!

PSALM 111:4-6 THE MESSAGE

SEPTEMBER 28

Some give freely, yet grow all the richer;
others withhold what is due, and only suffer
want. A generous person will be enriched,
and one who gives water will get water.

PROVERBS 11:24-25 NRSV

SEPTEMBER 29

Honor God with everything you own;
give him the first and the best.

PROVERBS 3:9 THE MESSAGE

SEPTEMBER 30

Praise the Lord! O give thanks to the Lord, for he is good; for his steadfast love endures forever. Who can utter the mighty doings of the Lord, or declare all his praise?

PSALM 106:1-2 NRSV

OCTOBER 1

I will praise you with an upright heart
as I learn your righteous laws. I will obey
your decrees; do not utterly forsake me.

PSALM 119:7-8 NIV

OCTOBER 2

I know that the Lord is great, that our Lord
is greater than all gods. The Lord does
whatever pleases him, in the heavens and
on the earth, in the seas and all their depths.
He makes clouds rise from the ends of the
earth; he sends lightning with the
rain and brings out the wind
from his storehouses.

PSALM 135:5-7 NIV

OCTOBER 3

The highest heavens belong to the Lord, but the earth he has given to man. It is not the dead who praise the Lord, those who go down to silence; it is we who extol the Lord, both now and forevermore. Praise the Lord.

PSALM 115:16-18 NIV

OCTOBER 4

The fruit of the righteous is a tree of life,
and he who wins souls is wise.

PROVERBS 11:30 NIV

OCTOBER 5

Taste and see that the Lord is good;
blessed is the man who takes refuge in him.
Fear the Lord, you his saints,
for those who fear him lack nothing.

PSALM 34:8-9 NIV

OCTOBER 6

Praise the Lord, all you nations;
extol him, all you peoples. For great
is his love toward us, and the faithfulness
of the Lord endures forever.

PSALM 117:1-2 NIV

OCTOBER 7

Give thanks to the Lord, call on his name;
make known among the nations what
he has done. Sing to him, sing praise to him;
tell of all his wonderful acts. Glory in his holy
name; let the hearts of those who seek
the Lord rejoice. Look to the Lord and his
strength; seek his face always.

PSALM 105:1-4 NIV

OCTOBER 8

By wisdom the Lord laid the earth's foundations, by understanding he set the heavens in place; by his knowledge the deeps were divided, and the clouds let drop the dew.

PROVERBS 3:19-20 NIV

OCTOBER 9

You, God, prescribed the right way to live;
now you expect us to live it.
Oh, that my steps might be steady,
keeping to the course you set.

PSALM 119:4-5 THE MESSAGE

OCTOBER 10

So I said: "Do not take me away,
O my God, in the midst of my days;
your years go on through all generations.
In the beginning you laid the foundations
of the earth, and the heavens are the work
of your hands. They will perish, but you
remain…. You remain the same, and your
years will never end. The children of your
servants will live in your presence."

PSALM 102:24-28 NIV

OCTOBER 11

But the steadfast love of the Lord
is from everlasting to everlasting
on those who fear him, and his
righteousness to children's children.

PSALM 103:17 NASB

OCTOBER 12

I will not be afraid of ten thousands
of people who have set themselves against
me all around. Arise, O Lord; save me,
O my God!… Salvation belongs to the Lord.
Your blessing is upon Your people.

PSALM 3:6-8 NKJV

OCTOBER 13

Whoever gives heed to instruction
prospers, and blessed is he
who trusts in the Lord.

PROVERBS 16:20 NIV

OCTOBER 14

He sends from heaven and saves me…
God sends his love and his faithfulness….
Be exalted, O God, above the heavens;
let your glory be over all the earth.

PSALM 57:3,5 NIV

OCTOBER 15

I will listen to what God the Lord will say;
he promises peace to his people, his saints—
but let them not return to folly. Surely his
salvation is near those who fear him,
that his glory may dwell in our land.

PSALM 85:8-9 NIV

OCTOBER 16

My soul is starved and hungry, raven-
ous!—insatiable for your nourishing commands.... Yes, your sayings on life are what
give me delight; I listen to them
as to good neighbors!

PSALM 119:20,24 THE MESSAGE

OCTOBER 17

Blessed is the nation whose God is the Lord,
the people he chose for his inheritance.
From heaven the Lord looks down and sees
all mankind; from his dwelling place
he watches all who live on earth—he who
forms the hearts of all, who considers
everything they do…. But the eyes
of the Lord are on those who fear him,
on those whose hope is in his unfailing love.

PSALM 33:12-15,18 NIV

OCTOBER 18

Hear, my child, and accept my words,
that the years of your life may be many.
I have taught you the way of wisdom;
I have led you in the paths of uprightness.

PROVERBS 4:10-11 NRSV

OCTOBER 19

To you I call, O Lord my Rock; do not turn a deaf ear to me. For if you remain silent, I will be like those who have gone down to the pit. Hear my cry for mercy as I call to you for help, as I lift up my hands toward your Most Holy Place.

PSALM 28:1-2 NIV

OCTOBER 20

The Lord is in his holy temple; the Lord is on his heavenly throne. He observes the sons of men; his eyes examine them.

PSALM 11:4 NIV

OCTOBER 21

I sought the Lord, and he answered me;
he delivered me from all my fears. Those who
look to him are radiant; their faces are never
covered with shame…. The angel of the
Lord encamps around those who fear him,
and he delivers them.

PSALM 34:4-7 NIV

OCTOBER 22

Let all the earth fear the Lord;
let all the people of the world revere him.
For he spoke, and it came to be;
he commanded, and it stood firm.

PSALM 33:8-9 NIV

OCTOBER 23

Shout with joy to God, all the earth!
Sing the glory of his name; make his praise
glorious! Say to God, "How awesome
are your deeds! So great is your power that
your enemies cringe before you. All the earth
bows down to you; they sing praise to you,
they sing praise to your name."

PSALM 66:1-4 NIV

OCTOBER 24

An anxious heart weighs a man down,
but a kind word cheers him up.

PROVERBS 12:25 NIV

OCTOBER 25

He waters the mountains from his upper chambers; the earth is satisfied by the fruit of his work. He makes grass grow for the cattle, and plants for man to cultivate— bringing forth food from the earth: wine that gladdens the heart of man, oil to make his face shine, and bread that sustains his heart.

PSALM 104:13-15 NIV

OCTOBER 26

I will praise you, O Lord, with all my heart;
I will tell of all your wonders. I will be glad
and rejoice in you; I will sing praise to your
name, O Most High.

PSALM 9:1-2 NIV

OCTOBER 27

Let them give thanks to the Lord for his
unfailing love and his wonderful deeds
for men. Let them sacrifice thank offerings
and tell of his works with songs of joy.

PSALM 107:21-22 NIV

OCTOBER 28

Be generous with me and I'll live a full life;
not for a minute will I take my eyes off
your road. Open my eyes so I can see what
you show me of your miracle-wonders.
I'm a stranger in these parts;
give me clear directions.

PSALM 119:17-19 THE MESSAGE

OCTOBER 29

It is better to take refuge in the Lord than to trust in man. It is better to take refuge in the Lord than to trust in princes.

PSALM 118:8-9 NIV

OCTOBER 30

When you walk, your step will not be hampered; and if you run, you will not stumble. Keep hold of instruction; do not let go; guard her, for she is your life.

PROVERBS 4:12-13 NRSV

OCTOBER 31

Let those who love the Lord hate evil,
for he guards the lives of his faithful ones
and delivers them from the hand
of the wicked. Light is shed upon
the righteous and joy on the upright in heart.
Rejoice in the Lord, you who are righteous,
and praise his holy name.

PSALM 97:10-12 NIV

NOVEMBER 1

Come, let's shout praises to God,
raise the roof for the Rock who saved us!
Let's march into his presence singing praises,
lifting the rafters with our hymns!

PSALM 95:1-2 THE MESSAGE

NOVEMBER 2

God has ascended amid shouts of joy,
the Lord amid the sounding of trumpets.
Sing praises to God, sing praises;
sing praises to our King, sing praises.

PSALM 47:5-6 NIV

NOVEMBER 3

My soul will rejoice in the Lord
and delight in his salvation.
My whole being will exclaim,
"Who is like you, O Lord?
You rescue the poor from those
too strong for them, the poor
and needy from those who rob them."

PSALM 35:9-10 NIV

NOVEMBER 4

A wife of noble character who can find?
She is worth far more than rubies.
Her husband has full confidence in her
and lacks nothing of value. She brings
him good, not harm, all the days of her life.

PROVERBS 31:10-12 NIV

NOVEMBER 5

Blessed is he whose transgressions
are forgiven, whose sins are covered.
Blessed is the man whose sin
the Lord does not count against him
and in whose spirit is no deceit.

PSALM 32:1-2 NIV

NOVEMBER 6

You brought me out of the womb;
you made me trust in you even at
my mother's breast. From birth I was cast
upon you; from my mother's womb you have
been my God. Do not be far from me,
for trouble is near and there is
no one to help.

PSALM 22:9-11 NIV

NOVEMBER 7

The Lord is a refuge for the oppressed,
a stronghold in times of trouble.
Those who know your name will trust in
you, for you, Lord, have never forsaken
those who seek you.

PSALM 9:9-10 NIV

NOVEMBER 8

Mark well that God doesn't miss a move
you make; he's aware of every step you take.

PROVERBS 5:21 THE MESSAGE

NOVEMBER 9

Cleanse me with hyssop, and I will be
clean; wash me, and I will be whiter than
snow. Let me hear joy and gladness;
let the bones you have crushed rejoice. Hide
your face from my sins and blot
out all my iniquity.

PSALM 51:7-9 NIV

NOVEMBER 10

Your ways, O God, are holy. What god
is so great as our God? You are the God who
performs miracles; you display your power
among the peoples. With your mighty
arm you redeemed your people.

PSALM 77:13-15 NIV

NOVEMBER 11

I have chosen the way of truth; I have set
my heart on your laws. I hold fast to your
statutes, O Lord; do not let me be put
to shame. I run in the path of your
commands, for you have set my heart free.

PSALM 119:30-32 NIV

NOVEMBER 12

O Lord, the God who saves me, day and night I cry out before you. May my prayer come before you; turn your ear to my cry.

PSALM 88:1-2 NIV

NOVEMBER 13

Perfume and incense bring joy to the heart,
and the pleasantness of one's friend springs
from his earnest counsel.

PROVERBS 27:9 NIV

NOVEMBER 14

Among the gods there is none like you,
O Lord; no deeds can compare with yours.
All the nations you have made will come and
worship before you, O Lord; they will bring
glory to your name. For you are great and
do marvelous deeds; you alone are God.

PSALM 86:8-10 NIV

NOVEMBER 15

We give thanks to you, O God…. You say, "I choose the appointed time; it is I who judge uprightly. When the earth and all its people quake, it is I who hold its pillars firm."

PSALM 75:1-3 NIV

NOVEMBER 16

For with you is the fountain of life;
in your light we see light. Continue your
love to those who know you,
your righteousness to the upright in heart.

PSALM 36:9-10 NIV

NOVEMBER 17

My child, keep your father's
commandment, and do not forsake
your mother's teaching. Bind them upon
your heart always; tie them around your
neck. When you walk, they will lead you;
when you lie down, they will watch over you;
and when you awake, they will talk with you.
For the commandment is a lamp
and the teaching a light, and the reproofs
of discipline are the way of life.

PROVERBS 6:20-23 NRSV

NOVEMBER 18

Do not cast me from your presence
or take your Holy Spirit from me. Restore
to me the joy of your salvation and grant
me a willing spirit, to sustain me.

PSALM 51:11-12 NIV

NOVEMBER 19

The righteous cry out, and the Lord hears them; he delivers them from all their troubles. The Lord is close to the brokenhearted and saves those who are crushed in spirit.

PSALM 34:17-18 NIV

NOVEMBER 20

Worship the Lord with gladness; come into his presence with singing. Know that the Lord is God. It is he that made us, and we are his; we are his people, and the sheep of his pasture. Enter his gates with thanksgiving, and his courts with praise. Give thanks to him, bless his name.

PSALM 100:2-4 NRSV

NOVEMBER 21

How can a young person live a clean life?
By carefully reading the map of your Word.
I'm single-minded in pursuit of you; don't
let me miss the road signs you've posted.
I've banked your promises in the vault
of my heart so I won't sin myself bankrupt.
Be blessed, God; train me in your
ways of wise living.

PSALM 119:9-12 THE MESSAGE

NOVEMBER 22

Many a man claims to have unfailing love,
but a faithful man who can find?
The righteous man leads a blameless life;
blessed are his children after him.

PROVERBS 20:6-7 NIV

NOVEMBER 23

Give thanks to the Lord, for he is good.
His love endures forever. Give thanks
to the God of gods. His love endures forever.
Give thanks to the Lord of lords: His love
endures forever. To him who alone does
great wonders, his love endures forever.

PSALM 136:1-4 NIV

NOVEMBER 24

He who dwells in the shelter of the Most
High will rest in the shadow of the Almighty.
I will say of the Lord, "He is my refuge
and my fortress, my God, in whom I trust."

PSALM 91:1-2 NIV

NOVEMBER 25

I am under vows to you, O God;
I will present my thank offerings to you.
For you have delivered me from death
and my feet from stumbling, that I may walk
before God in the light of life.

PSALM 56:12-13 NIV

NOVEMBER 26

The Lord foils the plans of the nations;
he thwarts the purposes of the peoples.
But the plans of the Lord stand
firm forever, the purposes of his heart
through all generations.

PSALM 33:10-11 NIV

NOVEMBER 27

God, teach me lessons for living
so I can stay the course. Give me insight
so I can do what you tell me—my whole
life one long, obedient response.

PSALM 119:33-34 THE MESSAGE

NOVEMBER 28

God is the King of all the earth;
sing to him a psalm of praise. God reigns
over the nations; God is seated on his holy
throne. The…kings of the earth belong
to God; he is greatly exalted.

PSALM 47:7-9 NIV

NOVEMBER 29

He who is kind to the poor lends
to the Lord, and he will reward him
for what he has done.

PROVERBS 19:17 NIV

NOVEMBER 30

I will praise you, O Lord, among the nations;
I will sing of you among the peoples.
For great is your love, reaching to the heavens; your faithfulness reaches to the skies.
Be exalted, O God, above the heavens;
let your glory be over all the earth.

PSALM 57:9-11 NIV

DECEMBER 1

O my Strength, I watch for you;
you, O God, are my fortress,
my loving God. God will go before me.

Psalm 59:9-10 NIV

DECEMBER 2

He alone is my rock and my salvation;
he is my fortress, I will not be shaken.
My salvation and my honor depend on God;
he is my mighty rock, my refuge.
Trust in him at all times, O people; pour out
your hearts to him, for God is our refuge.

PSALM 62:6-8 NIV

DECEMBER 3

My child, keep my words and store
up my commandments with you;
keep my commandments and live,
keep my teachings as the apple of your eye;
bind them on your fingers, write them
on the tablet of your heart.

PROVERBS 7:1-3 NRSV

DECEMBER 4

Yet I am always with you; you hold me
by my right hand. You guide me
with your counsel, and afterward
you will take me into glory.

PSALM 73:23-24 NIV

DECEMBER 5

Your righteousness reaches to the skies,
O God, you who have done great things.
Who, O God, is like you? Though you have
made me see troubles, many and bitter,
you will restore my life again; from the
depths of the earth you will
again bring me up.

PSALM 70:19-20 NIV

DECEMBER 6

The Lord reigns, let the earth be glad;
let the distant shores rejoice. Clouds and
thick darkness surround him; righteousness
and justice are the foundation of his throne.

PSALM 97:1-2 NIV

DECEMBER 7

May your unfailing love come to me,
O Lord, your salvation according to your
promise; then I will answer the one who
taunts me, for I trust in your word.

PSALM 119:41-42 NIV

DECEMBER 8

Smart people know how
to hold their tongue; their grandeur
is to forgive and forget.

PROVERBS 19:11 THE MESSAGE

DECEMBER 9

"Because he loves me," says the Lord, "I will rescue him; I will protect him, for he acknowledges my name. He will call upon me, and I will answer him; I will be with him in trouble, I will deliver him and honor him. With long life will I satisfy him and show him my salvation."

PSALM 91:14-16 NIV

DECEMBER 10

But as for me, I will always have hope; I will praise you more and more. My mouth will tell of your righteousness, of your salvation all day long, though I know not its measure.

PSALM 70:14-15 NIV

DECEMBER 11

The seas have lifted up, O Lord, the seas have lifted up their voice; the seas have lifted up their pounding waves. Mightier than the thunder of the great waters, mightier than the breakers of the sea— the Lord on high is mighty.

PSALM 93:3-4 NIV

DECEMBER 12

Choose my instruction instead of silver,
knowledge rather than choice gold,
for wisdom is more precious than rubies,
and nothing you desire can
compare with her.

PROVERBS 8:10-11 NIV

DECEMBER 13

How lovely is your dwelling place,
O Lord Almighty! My soul yearns, even
faints, for the courts of the Lord; my heart
and my flesh cry out for the living God.

PSALM 84:1-2 NIV

DECEMBER 14

You're the closest of all to me, God,
and all your judgments true. I've known
all along from the evidence of your words
that you meant them to last forever.

PSALM 119:151-152 THE MESSAGE

DECEMBER 15

Turn to me and have mercy on me; grant your strength to your servant and save the son of your maidservant. Give me a sign of your goodness, that my enemies may see it and be put to shame, for you, O Lord, have helped me and comforted me.

PSALM 86:16-17 NIV

DECEMBER 16

There is surely a future hope for you,
and your hope will not be cut off.

PROVERBS 23:18 NIV

DECEMBER 17

I will sing of the Lord's great love forever;
with my mouth I will make your faithfulness
known through all generations. I will declare
that your love stands firm forever, that you
established your faithfulness in heaven itself.

PSALM 89:1-2 NIV

DECEMBER 18

We give thanks to You, O God,
we give thanks! For Your wondrous
works declare that Your name is near.

PSALM 75:1 NKJV

DECEMBER 19

Within your temple, O God,
we meditate on your unfailing love.
Like your name, O God, your praise
reaches to the ends of the earth; your right
hand is filled with righteousness.

PSALM 48:9-10 NIV

DECEMBER 20

May my lips overflow with praise,
for you teach me your decrees.
May my tongue sing of your word,
for all your commands are righteous.
May your hand be ready to help me,
for I have chosen your precepts.
I long for your salvation, O Lord,
and your law is my delight.

DECEMBER 21

Whom have I in heaven but you?
And there is nothing on earth that I desire
other than you. My flesh and my heart
may fail, but God is the strength
of my heart and my portion forever.

PSALM 73:25-26

DECEMBER 22

The path of the righteous is like
the first gleam of dawn, shining ever
brighter till the full light of day.

PROVERBS 4:18 NIV

DECEMBER 23

Sunrise breaks through the darkness for good people—God's grace and mercy and justice! The good person is generous and lends lavishly; no shuffling or stumbling around for this one, but a sterling and solid and lasting reputation.... They lavish gifts on the poor—a generosity that goes on, and on, and on. An honored life! A beautiful life!

PSALM 112:4-6,9 THE MESSAGE

DECEMBER 24

The heavens praise your wonders,
O Lord, your faithfulness too, in the assembly
of the holy ones…. O Lord God Almighty,
who is like you? You are mighty, O Lord,
and your faithfulness surrounds you.

PSALM 89:5,8 NIV

DECEMBER 25

Sing to God, sing praise to his name,
extol him who rides on the clouds—his name
is the Lord—and rejoice before him.
A father to the fatherless, a defender
of widows, is God in his holy dwelling.
God sets the lonely in families.

PSALM 68:4-6 NIV

DECEMBER 26

The Lord reigns, he is robed in majesty;
the Lord is robed in majesty and is armed
with strength. The world is firmly established; it cannot be moved. Your throne
was established long ago;
you are from all eternity.

PSALM 93:1-3 NIV

DECEMBER 27

Be good to your servant, God; be as good
as your Word. Train me in good common
sense; I'm thoroughly committed to living
your way. Before I learned to answer you,
I wandered all over the place,
but now I'm in step with your Word.
You are good, and the source of good;
train me in your goodness.

PSALM 119:65-68 THE MESSAGE

DECEMBER 28

The righteous man walks in his integrity;
his children are blessed after him.

PROVERBS 20:7 NKJV

DECEMBER 29

Teach me your way, O Lord, and I will walk in your truth; give me an undivided heart, that I may fear your name. I will praise you, O Lord my God, with all my heart; I will glorify your name forever.

PSALM 86:11-12 NIV

DECEMBER 30

I wait for the Lord, my soul waits,
and in his word I put my hope.
My soul waits for the Lord more
than watchmen wait for the morning,
more than watchmen wait for the morning.

PSALM 130:5-6 NIV

DECEMBER 31